headwork reading

Thanks but No Thanks

and Spit in My Eye

Chris Culshaw

Oxford University Press

Zippy
CORN

Thanks But No Thanks

1
Please Don't Feed the Animals

'Paul!'

No answer.

'Paul – time you were up.'

No answer.

'Paul! If you're not down here in five minutes... No breakfast!'

Paul Turner's mother smiled as she heard him jump out of bed and run downstairs. A few minutes later he was starting his fifth bowl of cornflakes. Mrs Turner picked up the empty packet and shook it: 'Trying to eat your way into the Guinness Book of Records?'

Paul didn't answer.

After breakfast Paul's mother asked him to go down to the paper shop. 'Tell Vera that we got the *Mail* yesterday. I wanted the *Mirror*. It's that new paper girl, Sophie what's-her-name. She's a real bird-brain.'

Paul pulled on his jacket and trainers. 'Will I need any money?'

'No, the bill's been paid.'

'Are you sure, mum?'

'Sure I'm sure and before you ask – no, you can't get any sweets. You've had your pocket money this week.'

Paul ran down the front path. Just outside the garden gate he tripped over a supermarket trolley and fell into the gutter. He tried to stand up but could not because his right foot was stuck behind the little plastic seat at the back of the trolley.

He was still hopping about when his friend, Stuart, came along. 'Give me a hand, Stu,' said Paul.

'Don't you mean, "Give me a foot"?' said his friend, doing nothing to help him.

Paul fell backwards into the hedge and ended up underneath the trolley. Stu said, 'You look just like Sunshine, my pet hamster.' He bent down and pushed a finger through the bars of the trolley. Paul tried to bite it.

Stu said, 'This reminds me of that school trip to Chester Zoo. All those signs saying "Please Don't Feed the Animals".'

'Very funny, Stuart,' said Paul, pulling a leaf out of his ear. 'Are you going to give me a hand or not?'

2
A Reward?

When Stuart and Paul got back from the paper shop, Mrs Turner was standing at the front gate looking at the trolley. 'Who's left this here?' she said crossly.

Paul said, 'I don't know.'

'Well, it can't stay here,' she went on. 'I need you to do a bit of shopping. You can take it back when you go.'

Paul looked at his friend. 'But... er... Stu's come round to... er... help me with some homework, haven't you, Stu?'

Stu frowned. 'Have I? Oh... yeah... right. Homework, sure.'

Mrs Turner knew they weren't telling the truth. She looked at her son and grinned. 'They might give you a reward,' she said.

'Who?' said Paul.

'The supermarket,' replied his mother. 'These trolleys are worth a lot of money.' She took out her purse. 'Here's a fiver. Get me some potatoes, bread, and some milk.'

Paul put the money in his back pocket. 'Can me and Stu get an ice cream?'

His mother tried not to laugh, 'Alright, if there's any change. But make sure you're back for lunch.'

3
Hardy's Lucky Day

Near Stuart's house they met Stuart's dad. He was taking Hardy, their dog, for a walk. Hardy was a large black labrador. He jumped up at Paul and licked his face.

When the two boys told Stuart's dad where they were going, he smiled. He tied Hardy's lead to the trolley handle and said, 'It's your lucky day, Hardy. Stuart's going to take you for a nice long walk.'

The trolley had a mind of its own. It was impossible to push it in a straight line. It kept crashing into lamp-posts and running off the pavement into the gutter. One of the wheels squeaked like a dentist's drill.

'That squeak's driving me mad,' said Stuart crossly. 'How much further?'

'About half a mile.'

'Half a mile!'

'It will be worth it! They're not going to give us a reward for pushing this trolley a few yards, are they? When we tell them how far we've pushed this thing they'll probably give us a fiver. Maybe more.'

'Are you sure?'

'Yeah. You heard what my mum said and she's never wrong about money.'

Stuart's face lit up. 'Hey, we could tell them we found it in... er... London... and we've pushed it all the way up the M1. How much would they give us then?'

Paul shook his head slowly. 'Not a lot, Stu. Not a lot.'

4

Dog Power

Ten minutes later they were passing some shops when Paul stopped and said, 'I've got an idea. Have you got any money, Stu?'

'Yeh, a quid. Why?'

'Lend it to me, will you?'

'What about your mum's fiver?'

'That's for the shopping. Come on, just lend me the quid. You'll get it back, honest.'

Stuart handed over the pound and Paul went into a sweet shop. He came out a few minutes later with a Mars bar. Then he went into a florist's shop and came out with a long, thin garden cane.

'What are you doing?' asked his friend.

'I don't know why I didn't think of this before.'

'Think of what?'

'Dog Power, Stu. Dog Power.'

Paul took the laces out of his trainers and used one lace to tie the cane to the trolley. He used the other lace to tie the Mars bar on to the end of the cane.

Next, he tied Hardy's lead on to the front of the trolley. The dog saw the Mars bar, jumped up and tried to get it. Stu, who was holding the trolley, was pulled off his feet.

Paul laughed, 'See what I mean, Stu? Dog Power!'

5
Guide Dog?

Hardy set off at great speed, with Paul and Stu hanging on by the skin of their teeth. Everything was fine until Hardy saw a cat outside the post office. Hardy was terrified of cats and ran a mile whenever he saw one. He took one look at this cat – a huge black-and-white tom – and ran for cover! He dragged the two boys across the street with him.

'Look out!' said Paul, 'he's heading for the chemist's!'

The double doors of the chemist's shop were wide open. 'I'll be safe in here,' thought Hardy, and in he went. He skidded to a halt by the counter. The assistant snapped, 'Can't you two read?' She pointed to a sign, 'No dogs, except guide dogs.' She looked at Hardy and scowled, 'That definitely doesn't look like a guide dog to me!'

The two boys struggled to get the trolley and Hardy out of the shop.

Stu was holding the trolley when he tripped and lost his grip of the handle. Hardy saw his chance and took off like a rocket.

'Come on,' shouted Paul, 'he's running the wrong way!'

6
Mush! Mush!

When they caught up with Hardy the trolley was upside down and the lead was twisted round a lamp-post. 'You silly dog,' said Stuart, 'you could have strangled yourself.'

'He's got too much Dog Power,' said Paul, as he turned the trolley over and checked the Mars bar was still in place. 'We've got to think of a way to slow him down.'

'I know,' said Stuart. 'Here – hold the handle tight.' He climbed into the trolley. It was a tight fit. His knees were pushed up under his chin and his arms were hanging down, on the outside.

'Come on, Hardy,' Stuart shouted, 'Mush! Mush!'

The dog did not move. He just looked up at Stuart and wagged his tail.

'Try waving the Mars bar near his nose,' said Paul. Stuart untied the cane and held it out like a fishing rod. He dangled the Mars bar inches away from Hardy's nose. The dog jumped at it and the trolley rolled forward. 'Go for it, Hardy!' shouted Paul and they were off.

7
Dead Leg

Stuart soon worked out how to steer the trolley. If he held the 'fishing rod' to the left, Hardy pulled to the left. If he held it to the right, the dog pulled to the right. They made their way past the bus station, across the market, through the sub-way, and into the car park behind the supermarket.

All of a sudden Stu shouted, 'Stop! I've got cramp. My left leg's gone dead. Quick, give me a hand to get out.'

Paul pulled hard on the handle and the trolley stopped. Stu stood up in the trolley and gave a loud cry of pain. Then he fell over, backwards. Paul let go of the handle of the trolley and tried to grab him.

Stuart's cry startled the dog and Hardy ran off in a panic, dragging the trolley with him. Stuart was still stuck in the trolley, hanging over the back of it. He was half-in and half-out, rather like a bonfire guy. Paul suddenly gasped in horror as the upside-down face of his friend disappeared between two vans which were parked nearby.

8

We're not Thieves

Paul didn't see what happened next. He heard an angry shout, Hardy barking, and a terrible clatter. He ran between the vans and found Stuart underneath the trolley with Hardy sitting next to him, eating the Mars bar. Nearby was a large pile of plastic bread trays. The pile moved – as if it were some strange creature. Then a very angry face appeared.

It was the driver of one of the vans. He had been collecting a stack of empty trays from the back of the supermarket, when he had been hit by a whirlwind called Hardy. He was struggling to his feet when a man in a smart grey suit came running over.

He was the manager of the supermarket and he said he was going to call the police. He thought Paul and Stuart were trying to steal the trolley. 'We lose dozens every week,' he said crossly. 'It costs the store a small fortune.'

'We weren't trying to nick it, honest,' said Paul nervously. 'We're not thieves. We found it and my mum said if we brought it back you'd give us a reward.'

The man looked at the boys and laughed. 'A reward? After what your dog's just done to my driver! You must be joking.'

9
Bad News Boys

Stuart started to panic. His mother would kill him if the manager called the police. 'But it's true.' He turned to the driver and said, 'Hardy's my dog and I'm sorry he knocked you down. He's pulled the trolley all the way from Leyland Road.'

The manager looked at the driver and grinned. The driver started to laugh. 'Did you say Leyland Road?' he asked, 'on the other side of the park?'

The boys nodded. The driver was shaking with laughter. He went over to the trolley and looked at the handle. 'Bad news, boys. This isn't one of ours. It's from Kwiksave.'

'Do you mean...' stammered Stuart.

'Afraid so,' said the manager, 'you'll have to take it all the way back to their Parkfield store.' He looked over at Hardy, who had finished the Mars bar and was looking round for more, and said, 'Take my advice – push it this time!'

Out Patients
Casualty

Spit in My Eye

1

Crazy Cathy

She was crazy, my sister Cathy. She drove my mum and dad wild. She was always in trouble and always doing mad, dangerous things.

My mum used to say, 'You're her big brother, Matthew. Big brothers have to look out for their little sisters. Take care of her.' I tried to stop her. But crazy Cathy would never listen to me.

She was like a cat with nine lives. She broke her arm – twice, then her leg, and two fingers all in the space of a year! Dad used to say, 'Cathy spends more time at that hospital than at home.' He was right. All the nurses knew Cathy's name. They used to say, 'Oh no. Here she is again! What is it this time?'

2

Matt the Mat

Cathy wanted to be a stunt woman when she was older. 'I'm going to be rich and famous,' she used to say dreamily.

I told her, 'Stunt women have to jump off sky-scrapers and fight sharks.'

Cathy just laughed, 'No problem, Matt. I fight you, don't I?'

She did too! She used to pull me onto the floor and trample all over me, saying, 'You are just like a mat, Matt.'

When I was eleven I went to the High School. I was a bit scared because I thought that I might get bullied. There were some tough kids there.

Cathy reassured me, 'Don't worry, Matt. If anyone tries to wipe their feet on you, I'll come up there and sort them out.'

3
Looking Back

Cathy and me are grown up now. We are both married and we both have our own kids. The other day I was looking at some old photos. Those photos brought back memories. I remembered some of the crazy things she used to do, like the stunts she did on her BMX bike.

She was ten when she got that bike. We had a high wall around our garden. It must have been at least two metres high. One day she lifted her bike on to the top of the wall and rode along the top of it. It was only a few centimetres wide. When dad saw her, he had a

fit. 'Get down off that wall immediately!' he shouted, 'you'll break your neck.' But she didn't fall. She even tried to get me to do it but I was too scared.

Yes, I have lots of photos of my sister. I like looking at them because they bring back all the happy times we had together. But there was one stunt that Cathy did that went badly wrong. It nearly cost her her life. There are no photos of that day...

4
The Challenge

The boy next door, Tom Hale, was the first to do it and he said, 'I bet nobody else can do it.'

Of course, as soon as Cathy heard about the stunt she just had to try it. Tom laughed and said, 'You'll never do it. Not on your old wreck of a bike.'

So Cathy wanted to borrow my bike. I said, 'No way! It'll end up in the canal.' But she kept going on at me until I gave in.

There was an old barge on the canal. Across the back of the barge was a wide wooden plank sticking out over the canal – a bit like a diving board. There was a two-metre gap between the end of the plank and the other side of the canal. The challenge was to get across that gap on the bike.

Tom Hale showed Cathy how it was done.

He rode very fast along the tow-path, raced along the plank, flew off the end, and landed with a thump on the far side of the canal.

'A piece of cake,' said Cathy.

5
It's Not So Funny

Maybe she was going too slow. Maybe the bike was too heavy for her. I don't know. She flew off the end of the plank but she didn't reach the other side and fell back into the water. My bike came down on top of her.

At first we all laughed because it looked funny – like a circus act. I just waited. 'Crazy Cathy will bob up like a cork,' I thought. 'She'll just climb out and have another go.'

But Cathy didn't bob up. The laughter stopped and I started to panic. A voice in my head was saying, 'It's all your fault. You let her borrow your bike and now she's dead.'

Tom Hale, his face white with fear, jumped into the canal. He dived down, grabbed

Cathy's hair, and pulled her head out of the water. Shocked into action, I jumped in to help him. He gasped, 'She's stuck. She's tangled up in your bike.'

I ducked under, grabbed hold of the bike and heaved it up. Cathy's foot was trapped in the frame. I pulled her shoe off and she was free. We dragged her up onto the canal path. Tom looked really scared, 'Is she....?'

6
A is for Airways

I think I saved her life. I'll never know for sure. We had done some first aid at school. The 'ABC' rule. My mind went blank. 'A is for what? Please God, help me remember. A is for what? A is for what? A is for airways! That's it, A is for airways.'

I opened Cathy's mouth – it was full of muddy weed. I cleared it out with my finger and put her head on one side. I did my best to open her airways. Then I put my face next to hers. Was she breathing? Was she alive? Suddenly, she coughed up a mouthful of dirty canal water right in my face. She was alive!

Cathy did not become a stunt woman after all. She left school, went to college and now she is a nurse.

We often talk about that day, Cathy and me. We laugh about it now. I say, 'To think I risked my life to save you, and what did you do? Just spit in my eye! Some sister!'

Great Clarendon Street, Oxford, OX2 6DP

Oxford University Press is a department of the University of Oxford.
It furthers the University's objective of excellence in research, scholarship,
and education by publishing worldwide in

Oxford New York

Athens Auckland Bangkok Bogotá Buenos Aires Calcutta
Cape Town Chennai Dar es Salaam Delhi Florence Hong Kong Istanbul
Karachi Kuala Lumpur Madrid Melbourne Mexico City Mumbai
Nairobi Paris São Paulo Shanghai Singapore Taipei Tokyo Toronto Warsaw

with associated companies in Berlin Ibadan

Oxford is a trade mark of Oxford University Press
in the UK and in certain other countries

First published 1995

Reprinted 1996, 1997, 2000

ISBN 0 19 833496 6

Printed in Great Britain

Illustrations by Jolyon Webb